AF349123

To Celebrate

____

____

Date

____

THANK YOU FOR COMING.

Guest Name

Wishes & Messages

Email/Phone

Guest Name

Wishes & Messages

Email/Phone

Guest Name

Wishes & Messages

Email/Phone

Guest Name

Wishes & Messages

Email/Phone

Guest Name

Wishes & Messages

Email/Phone

Guest Name

Wishes & Messages

Email/Phone

Guest Name

____

Wishes & Messages

____

____

____

____

____

____

____

Email/Phone

Guest Name

Wishes & Messages

Email/Phone

Guest Name

Wishes & Messages

Email/Phone

Guest Name

Wishes & Messages

Email/Phone

Guest Name

Wishes & Messages

Email/Phone

Guest Name

Wishes & Messages

Email/Phone

Guest Name

Wishes & Messages

Email/Phone

Guest Name

Wishes & Messages

Email/Phone

Guest Name

Wishes & Messages

Email/Phone

Guest Name

Wishes & Messages

Email/Phone

Guest Name

Wishes & Messages

Email/Phone

Guest Name

Wishes & Messages

Email/Phone

Guest Name

Wishes & Messages

Email/Phone

Guest Name

Wishes & Messages

Email/Phone

Guest Name

____

Wishes & Messages

____

____

____

____

____

____

Email/Phone

Guest Name

Wishes & Messages

Email/Phone

Guest Name

Wishes & Messages

Guest Name

Wishes & Messages

Email/Phone

Guest Name

Wishes & Messages

Email/Phone

Guest Name

____

Wishes & Messages

____

____

____

____

____

____

Email/Phone

Guest Name

Wishes & Messages

Email/Phone

Guest Name

____

Wishes & Messages

____

____

____

____

____

____

Email/Phone

Guest Name

Wishes & Messages

Email/Phone

Guest Name

____

Wishes & Messages

____

____

____

____

____

____

____

Email/Phone

Guest Name

Wishes & Messages

Email/Phone

Guest Name

Wishes & Messages

Email/Phone

Guest Name

Wishes & Messages

Email/Phone

Guest Name

Wishes & Messages

Email/Phone

Guest Name

Wishes & Messages

Email/Phone

Guest Name

Wishes & Messages

Email/Phone

Guest Name

Wishes & Messages

Email/Phone

Guest Name

____

Wishes & Messages

____

____

____

____

____

____

Email/Phone

Guest Name

Wishes & Messages

Email/Phone

Guest Name

Wishes & Messages

Email/Phone

Guest Name

Wishes & Messages

EMAIL/PHONE

Guest Name

Wishes & Messages

Email/Phone

Guest Name

Wishes & Messages

____

____

____

____

____

____

Email/Phone

Guest Name

Wishes & Messages

Email/Phone

Guest Name

Wishes & Messages

Email/Phone

Guest Name

Wishes & Messages

Email/Phone

Guest Name

Wishes & Messages

EMAIL/PHONE

Guest Name

Wishes & Messages

Email/Phone

Guest Name

____

Wishes & Messages

____

____

____

____

____

____

Email/Phone

Guest Name

Wishes & Messages

Email/Phone

Guest Name

Wishes & Messages

Email/Phone

Guest Name

Wishes & Messages

Email/Phone

Guest Name

Wishes & Messages

Email/Phone

Guest Name

Wishes & Messages

Email/Phone

Guest Name

Wishes & Messages

Email/Phone

Guest Name

Wishes & Messages

Email/Phone

Guest Name

Wishes & Messages

Email/Phone

Guest Name

____

Wishes & Messages

____

____

____

____

____

____

Email/Phone

Guest Name

Wishes & Messages

EMAIL/PHONE

Guest Name

Wishes & Messages

Email/Phone

Guest Name

Wishes & Messages

EMAIL/PHONE

Guest Name

____

Wishes & Messages

____

____

____

____

____

____

Email/Phone

Guest Name

Wishes & Messages

Email/Phone

Guest Name

____

Wishes & Messages

____

____

____

____

____

____

Email/Phone

Guest Name

Wishes & Messages

Email/Phone

Guest Name

Wishes & Messages

Email/Phone

Guest Name

Wishes & Messages

Email/Phone

Guest Name

Wishes & Messages

Email/Phone

Guest Name

Wishes & Messages

Email/Phone

Guest Name

Wishes & Messages

Email/Phone

Guest Name

Wishes & Messages

Email/Phone

Guest Name

Wishes & Messages

Email/Phone

Guest Name

Wishes & Messages

Email/Phone

Guest Name

Wishes & Messages

Email/Phone

Guest Name

Wishes & Messages

EMAIL/PHONE

Guest Name

Wishes & Messages

Email/Phone

Guest Name

Wishes & Messages

Email/Phone

Guest Name

Wishes & Messages

Email/Phone

Guest Name

____

Wishes & Messages

____

____

____

____

____

____

Email/Phone

Guest Name

Wishes & Messages

Email/Phone

Guest Name

____

Wishes & Messages

____

____

____

____

____

____

Email/Phone

Guest Name

Wishes & Messages

Email/Phone

Guest Name

Wishes & Messages

Email/Phone

Guest Name

Wishes & Messages

Email/Phone

Guest Name

Wishes & Messages

Email/Phone

Guest Name

Wishes & Messages

Email/Phone

Guest Name

Wishes & Messages

Email/Phone

Guest Name

Wishes & Messages

Email/Phone

Guest Name

____

Wishes & Messages

____

____

____

____

____

____

Email/Phone

Guest Name

Wishes & Messages

EMAIL/PHONE

Guest Name

Wishes & Messages

Email/Phone

Guest Name

Wishes & Messages

Email/Phone

Guest Name

Wishes & Messages

Email/Phone

Guest Name

Wishes & Messages

Email/Phone

Guest Name

Wishes & Messages

EMAIL/PHONE

Guest Name

Wishes & Messages

Email/Phone

Guest Name

____

Wishes & Messages

____

____

____

____

____

____

Email/Phone

Guest Name

Wishes & Messages

Email/Phone

Guest Name

Wishes & Messages

Email/Phone

Guest Name

Wishes & Messages

Email/Phone

Guest Name

Wishes & Messages

Email/Phone

Guest Name

Wishes & Messages

Email/Phone

Guest Name

Wishes & Messages

Email/Phone

Guest Name

Wishes & Messages

Email/Phone

Guest Name

Wishes & Messages

Email/Phone

NOTES & PHOTOS

NOTES & PHOTOS

NOTES & PHOTOS

NOTES & PHOTOS

NOTES & PHOTOS

GIFT LOG

Name /Email /Phone

Gift

GIFT LOG

Name /Email /Phone	Gift

GIFT LOG

Name / Email / Phone	Gift

GIFT LOG

Name / Email / Phone   Gift

GIFT LOG

Name / Email / Phone	Gift

GIFT LOG

Name /Email /Phone

Gift

GIFT LOG

Name / Email / Phone	Gift